Beauty for Ashes

A Journey of Healing

Emma Leigh Levine

ISBN 979-8-89243-115-6 (paperback)
ISBN 979-8-89243-116-3 (digital)

Christian Faith Publishing
832 Park Avenue
Meadville, PA 16335
www.christianfaithpublishing.com

Printed in the United States of America

*To Chelsey G., who faithfully stood by me and pointed
me to Jesus throughout this long journey of healing*

*To Kelsey H., who refused to allow me to believe I
was "just crazy" no matter how much I begged her
to; instead, she listened and encouraged me*

*To Lori T., who enthusiastically said, "Let's EMDR
it" after I would tell her a false belief*

Contents

A Note to the Reader

Dear reader,

A lot of these poems, especially at the beginning, come with a trigger warning. Please take that seriously!

I grew up in a small town in West Virginia. Until I became a Christian myself, I claimed to grow up in a Christian home. My family went to church, but things were a lot different behind closed doors. This is especially true about my dad. He helped baptize me but also committed evil against me. Throughout my life, he has continually disrespected my physical boundaries, made perverted comments about my body, touched me, and made me touch him. Unfortunately, people can get physical traits from their parents. My dad's family all have a bend at the top of their ear. He passed this down to me. Because of this similarity, sometimes seeing myself reminded me of my abuser.

This chapbook began as a way for me to cope and heal. I wrote many of these poems at various points during Christian counseling and EMDR, which took about three years. While my story is interwoven with trauma, it is ultimately one of redemption because of Jesus's love for me and work in my life! My hope is that God will use these poems in the lives of others in any way He sees fit. My dream is to become a Christian counselor and help others find redemption in Christ, just like I did!

Love always,
Emma Leigh Levine

Part 1

The Darkness

Searching for Hope

Where can you find hope?
Can it be bought in a store?
Maybe you can plunder through your pockets
To find enough
Change
What does hope cost?
Is it a million dollars
Or a million memories
Do people search their whole lives for it?
Maybe it can be borrowed
Like a pinch of salt for a soup recipe
And your next-door neighbor has some extra
And will be able to spare you
A bit
They say it can go a long way
You can possibly catch a glimpse
In the bright-blue eyes of a child
Who hasn't met her monsters yet
Perhaps her parents protected her
From dancing with their demons
I've heard you can see it
Scattered through the Good Book
But my fingertips are tender
From flipping through the pages
Of my grandfather's Bible
So where can you find hope?
If you figure it out, please let me know!

Satan's Playbook

Sometimes I wake from a sound sleep
To Satan whispering into my ear
He always starts by saying my abuse
Was my fault, so I start to think
You know, sometimes I was a bad kid
My room has been a mess
And I have thrown a few fits
Maybe I did have fault in this
"You could have stopped it if you wanted to
But you went along with everything he did"
I start to wrestle with the things I could have done
But my mouth didn't move, and my body laid limp
I wish I'd have had the strength to fight
So like a spider spins his web
Satan keeps spinning those thoughts in my head
"What kind of daughter are you?"
I guess I don't deserve love from my father
Was I born unlovable, or was it something I did
To render myself not good enough for him?
By this time, I start to pick up Satan's slack
'Cause common sense says that if I don't deserve love from my dad
Then I don't deserve it from other people
And since I don't deserve love, then I must
Deserve evil
So I'm left longing for the love
I am ultimately unworthy of
And I cling tightly to the words of the guys
That say "I love you" more times than they say "Lose some weight"
It's just a bruise here and there
You see, the mirror is Satan's minion

As my foundation starts to blend with that purple-and-blue dot
I can hear him loud and clear
"Your body is bad. It will never be clean!"
Despite the EXPO-marker Bible verses
On that mirror, deep down I believe him
So over and over, I wash my hands, and as those suds go down the
    sink
I remember how my innocence was washed away
"Don't forget that it felt good," Satan whispers
How could my own body betray me?
I try to make up for it with good deeds
But by this point, I am like a fly
Stuck in Satan's web of lies
Will I ever be free?

Gaslighting

"*Good* morning, my sweetheart
*A*re you ready for breakfast?"
*S*miling, he flips the French toast
*L*ike he didn't violate me seven hours ago
I guess it's fine? I
*G*uess dads can do that sort of thing?
"*H*ow did you sleep last night, honey?"
*T*hings seem to be in place, so
I add syrup to my breakfast, and we small-talk.
*N*o mention of last night, I'll just follow his lead.
*G*reat, I guess. He hardly ever cooks for me.

A Survivor's Prayer

Lord, is this what I am supposed to see
When I look at my reflection staring back at me
There is a bend in my left ear just like his
The size of my breasts is all I have to give
Shouldn't he want a man to know my heart?
When I look at my stomach, I flash back to the shower
My fingers gripping that frayed washcloth over it
At forty-six and twelve, I thought he had all the power
It doesn't matter how many times
I wash, rinse, and repeat
I stare at my soapy hands in the bathroom sink
And I can't stand knowing
They will never be clean
I try to hide from that with guys
A mask or alcoholic drinks
And I run even harder toward my degree
But I can never earn enough
For that shame to shrink
Every minute of the day, it follows me
And even at night, when I sleep
Images of his face still haunt my dreams
Now every man of God will run away
No one can kiss these lips
Without the bitter taste
Of being taught what was normal
In my first love's grips
Will there ever be a man equipped
That will be willing to handle that kind of pain
I live my life trying to avoid mirrors
Mastectomies cost too much

Each glance at my body
It is as if my boobs apologize in terror
And every time I see my butt
I am reminded of how it was touched
So I go to the gym in hopes of changing it
Maybe if I alter its appearance
I will be able to see clearer
But I'm not sure I will ever stop
Feeling his hands' clutch
Unfortunately, my friend familiarity keeps me near her
And the fear of changing all of this is my crutch
I don't even know who I'd be without these encounters
But, God, You had the power to create
The entire world with just words
Was I not worth it for You to speak?
Mom went on a trip with my sister alone
Couldn't You have worked it out so I could have gone?
Or allowing me to lock the door
Wouldn't have been that hard
God, just tell me why You didn't intervene!
Why did You choose not to protect Your daughter
From all of this pain?

Friends (Probably) with Good Intentions

Thank God for faithful friends
But sometimes it's a blessing
To sit in silence
With a loved one who is suffering

"God let this happen to you
So you could have empathy"
Oh, did He?
Because what it did to me
Was merely make my emotions numb
For several years
And apathy left me feeling
Unlike a human

"Don't share your burdens
They are too much for us to bear"
But I thought you cared?
I thought God's Word said
Our burdens are for one another to share
So I've learned to give them to Him
But the weight of sin gets heavy
Without some good friends

"You were fearfully and wonderfully made"
But don't you understand?
I was *made* over twenty years ago
And I am half a monster
Half of my blood comes from that man
My body is broken

It feels damaged and dirty
And now I'm just fearful~~ly and wonderfully made~~

"Just move on"
How can I explain
That's the worst path to take?
I know I believe lies
But I'm not sure of the truth
And Jesus doesn't seem to think I'm meant
To live my life this way

"You are just doing this for attention"
But not a single soul sees
My face at night
As warm tears flow down to my pillow
Like streams
And keep dampening it
Until I finally fall asleep

"Don't you just believe what God says about you?"
Well…I kind of do
But I'm just so confused
My whole life, my dad
Taught me that lies were the truth
So believing anything
Isn't as easy as it seems

"You are just messed up"
Perhaps I am
So maybe God will show me mercy

Thank God for faithful friends
But sometimes I just fake a smile
Because they don't know it's a blessing
To sit in silence
When a loved one is suffering

A Distressed Daughter
A Psalm of Lament

How long, oh Lord,
Will Your presence feel
Both inches and miles away from my heart?
Will a father's tender love and kindness
To me ever become real?
How long will my mirror
Remind me of abuse?
The body You made
Now the devil's distraction
Because it has been used
For his mere satisfaction.
Will I ever be the girl
That looks at her reflection
And simply sees someone who
Fearfully and wonderfully
Bears the image of You?
How long will I need
To seek friends for relief?
When the lies feel like
Shackles digging into my feet,
They faithfully remind me I'm free
And speaks Your truth into my unbelief.
Please, God, give them strength
To keep carrying me.
How many times will I see him in my dreams
And wake up to a reality worse than it seems?
Now too terrified to sleep.
So I stare at the popcorn ceiling,

Getting lost in the white,
Lying awake in the dead of the night.
How many more holidays, Tuesdays, and birthdays
Will end in envy and grief
When I see the daddy and his daughter
Walking down the street?
Lord, please fix my false belief
He took everything from me,
My worth, my future, and every ounce of dignity,
But those only come from You,
Divinely given unconditionally.
His sin against me can't take them away.
I've been washed by Jesus's blood.
Dad's sin can't leave a crimson stain.
I call You God, Abba, or Lord
Because it hurts to call You Father.
The pain and confusion that comes from that word,
I know You don't want for Your daughter.
Your promises are true even when I can't see
But this story *not* too dark for You to redeem.
How long will it take my soul to heal?
Only with time I can know.
But, Abba, I ask You,
"Tonight hold me close."

Part 2

The Dissonance

Fathers and Daughters

Father-daughter bonds
Are unlike anything else.
I sure hope that's true.

A Letter to My Daughter

My friend, don't forget I know your pain
I saw your hurt and shared your grief
Terrible things were done against Me too
But on the cross, you were worth it
For Me to follow through
Now with empathy I am your great high priest
And one day at a time, we will break every chain
I chose your body as My dwelling place
By the Father's hands, you were
Fearfully and wonderfully made
Not a single cell was His mistake
His fingers knit together the bend in your ear
Despite what you think, your heart is
the only thing that needs repair
When I look at you
I see no crimson stain
Neither your own sin nor his still remains there
I was nailed to the cross so that you would be free
My blood has washed all sin as white as snow
I don't want your past to determine where you go
You really can lay those sixteen sin-filled years at My feet
I intimately know that seven-year-old
You carefully layered walls around her
But she was never invisible to Me
Together you can be like that child I know
When the right man meets you, he will know you reflect Me
You'll be deeply loved and have no need to hide
On your darkest days, he will help you believe

Despite your story, you are still Mine
When Satan starts to whisper about the things you have seen
The man I send you will fight against those lies
And remind you your story has already been redeemed
But for now, just rest in being My bride

The Healing Heart
An Inner Dialogue

You are just crazy
It would be foolish to think
You did the best you could
You deserved what happened
Don't let anyone tell you that
There is hope for your future
I believe
Your story is too far from redemption
It is a simple lie that
You are incredibly strong
I hope you see the truth that
You should have done more
Don't believe anyone who says
It is okay
You didn't understand well enough
You are responsible
Let go of the belief that
Healing can come to your heart
(Now read it from the bottom up)

My Darkest Hour
Jesus's Perspective

Precious girl, only fourteen
Wondering where I was that night
Asking yourself if I had even seen
Or turned My face
As he stripped your innocence away
Leaving you wanting to hide from Me
That night, I was standing right by your side
And saw the confusion in your eyes
Racking your brain for how it was your sin
But, beloved, please don't believe that lie
You morphed into a shell of a person
Emotions numbed by his horrible deeds
But for you, I still felt it all
You couldn't yet, but I was able to grieve
My heart cried out, and I wept for you
I know someday you'll be ready to see
How deeply his sin impacted you
But his sin was committed against Me too
In time we can walk this road together
You can reach for My hand
Let Me show you
Yours has always been clean
So don't be afraid to come close
Your spirit draws away from Me
Because it feels like you were betrayed
But in time, I will help you see
It was never supposed to be this way
A daughter's hands are for holding

Learning, helping, or folding to pray
And never meant for such an evil thing
You are so much more than a body
But even it isn't stained
It's holy, the Spirit living inside
Carefully crafted, wonderfully made
I hope you soon realize
Not every man will use you this way
For their pleasure, then toss you aside
You can always cry out, "Abba Father!"
Despite what it feels like
He chose not to turn his face
But your dad is part of the reason I came
He is living his life as his own king
Blinded by darkness, unable to see the light
Not serving but seeking his selfish desires
But behind his smile is a man not truly free
Enslaved to his sin, he's unable to realize
The depth of the wounds
He self-inflicted that night
For a fleeting feeling of pleasure
He pulled farther from the Father
But you were a broken cistern
He can't be fulfilled by his daughter
God's righteous wrath will be placed on him
Unless he reaches his hand out for Me
Accepting I died and rose again
Providing the only way to atone for his sin
I pray for the Father to spare him the bitter cup
I pray for him, I drank it all on that tree

A Father's Love

You are just a stepping stone to get what I want
It would be foolish to think
My desire is to be close to you
It may be hard for you to understand, but
You are too small to matter to me
Let go of the belief that
I would lay down my life for you
Nothing can change the fact that
To me, your worth is based on what you do
It is a lie that
I will never stop pursuing you
I want you to realize that
You have made too many mistakes
Don't ever believe that
You can run to me
How many times have I proven
You have to work limitlessly to please me
You need to stop living like
You are my precious daughter
(Now read it from the bottom up)

The EMDR Specialist

The eyes of an EMDR specialist
Meet mine at the beginning of each session
They fix themselves on my tense arms and twitching toes
As together we revisit the evil that took place
They somehow sometimes see my story before I do
They light up when they see a glimmer of hope in mine
The ears of an EMDR specialist
Listen closely to the details of the darkness
As I disclose what my dad and I have done
Sometimes for the first time
They pick up on the pitch of my voice
Giving clues to my mental state
When I don't even know it yet
The lips of an EMDR specialist
Speak words of grief or disgust or life
They remind me I am doing great
And I am no longer in ninth grade
He is seven hours away
I am here, and I am safe
Sometimes they excuse my French
And even join me in calling out his bull crap
The hands of an EMDR specialist
Facilitate healing
By pressing buttons to form vibrations
From left to right to left to right
So those things aren't so scary anymore
Or by scraping off the imaginary sleeve
Of false guilt
In hopes that I don't have to leave
Her office with that feeling

The stomach of an EMDR specialist has to be strong
To swallow story after story
And not be destroyed
I know sometimes my own stomach
Strikes back after EMDR
It rumbles and tumbles and growls
Like it is somehow ahead of me
In this process of grief
The heart of an EMDR specialist
Does more than just pump blood
It loves the broken body in front of her
And meets each one exactly where they are
Despite getting paid, she has to count the costs
Of hearing trauma after trauma; can she really put it all in the box?
Or does she hug her daughter a little tighter
Because she heard of another daughter
Forced to fight in a fight
No parent would ever want their child to partake in?
Maybe an EMDR specialist should be called a magician
Because of the tricks up her sleeve
A simple "Focus on the pain" that breaks
The body's walls and allows it to share the secrets
It kept inside for years
My favorite trick is when she turns
The valley of the shadow of death
Into an office painted white with floral decor
The hues of blues and greens and purples hanging on the wall
Her next trick is naming every color in the room
Until my body remembers I am no longer fourteen
The magician has to plan her tricks
As she plans for the best of each session
What skills to be taught and words to be said
And envisions the future of the person in front of her
Without fear or panic and fully feeling every feeling
And she plans for her client to plunder
Because the abuser won't win every battle

So she plans what can be plundered after this victory
Or at least what can be taken back and given to the rightful owner
It's magic when slowly she releases
The teenage girl from her prison cell
Painted blue, green, and purple
And puts that 6' 2" man behind those bars
So my body believes that I am safe
He is not all-powerful, and he can't touch me
And after the magician's performance
Together we celebrate our success
That the girl once imprisoned to her past
Is finally free

Hands

As I glimpse at the hands of the clock
My chest gets tighter
With every second passing by
Sweat starts to form on my clammy hands
Dinner has to be done
By the time he gets home
Everything has to go as planned
Or else I'll feel the sting of the viper's venom
Spewing off his tongue
The hands that were meant for a gentle touch
Were the hands I dreaded to feel
Pressed against my bottom lip
My unsteady hand would once again be
Wiping away a bit of blood
My fate was in his hands
I remembered hearing of another set of hands
The hands that reached out to those
The world declared untouchable
And touched the hands
That were once withered
Making them now able to straighten out
The carpenter's calloused hands
Could be simply lifted to the sky
Giving thanks to the Father
He was able to multiply barely any food into too much
The fisherman's fingers were willing to pull
The faithless man
Who was then able to stand
Where no man had stood before
And those hands stretched out on a cross

Nailed there for a fourteen-year-old girl
Shattered and without hope
Sandwiched between the dresser and wall
He met me there
And my hand reached out for His
Now I am settled safely into my Father's hands
Holding me, they help me stand
Against myself, Satan, and every scheme of man
His hands knit me together
Before I was born
They crafted each part with purpose
Like I was the clay and He was the potter
His gentle hands lead me to still water
And when small hands start to tremble
His righteous right hand eases my fear
But I long to see the hands of my Creator
And feel the warmth of His fingers
As they wipe away my tears
That have flowed down my face
From the hands of my dad

Part 3

The Dawn

The Mirror Moments

When I look in the mirror
I can finally see
An image bearer of God
Just as You created me to be

    My eyes
Now reflect that I am alive
No longer trying to tell of a girl
Dead on the inside
They see the beauty God has created
Or soak up the sight of my niece's smile
Oh, what wonderful sights to see

    My ear
Is much more than the bend in it
It is even a quirk You uniquely gave me
I can merely use it to hear
The praises sang to Jesus
Or to listen to a grieving friend
As I draw her near

    My lips
Can speak of the way God has healed me
When I was broken and lost
They can share of the sacrifice
My Savior made on the cross
As He paid the ultimate price
For every sinner to be free

My stomach
Reminds me of God's good and gracious gifts of food
The *M* on my shirt tag doesn't bother me
It sometimes even brings me joy
That *M* was an once an *XS*
I'm no longer that girl
No longer without hope and depressed

My butt
Reminds me of those dark days
When I thought that if I could change my body
I could forget what it went through
But I could never outrun my past
Now my reflection is a reminder
That kind of pain doesn't last

My hand
I raise it in thanksgiving
Because I finally believe
That it, along with the rest of me
Is clean
And I know it has been redeemed
I am in control of its new beginning

My chest
Isn't all that I have to offer
And I am wise enough to know
A father shouldn't say that of his daughter
And how special can something be
To bond with and sustain the life
Of a precious baby?

So I look in the mirror and slowly breathe
I never thought I'd live to see the day
I would praise my Creator
For being fearfully and wonderfully made

Praise to a Christian Counselor

Finding a good counselor is like finding a needle in a haystack.
When I finally found one, it was such a blessing.
I felt secure enough not to hold back.
Together, we talked through what we'd be addressing.
I wanted to feel whole and live without so much fear.
She listened closely to the details I disclosed.
She sat with me in my pain, sometimes shedding a tear.
Every moment, her compassion and empathy showed.
Her desire was for this caterpillar to become a butterfly.
Gentle spirits like hers are hard to come by.

As time passed, I became like a cocoon.
Eventually, I learned that she was safe.
Then we were able to diligently work at becoming attuned
With my body, not feeling alienated from this space.
One day, I finally physically felt my feet on the floor.
Even when it felt small, she celebrated any success.
Her inflection at those moments helped me trust our rapport.
When I couldn't, she held fast to His faithfulness.
She tenderly pointed me to my Savior.
Her desire was for a heart change, not just behavioral.

Finally, with her help, I became like a butterfly.
My time with her could come to an end.
She's encouraged and taught me new skills to apply.
She was a counselor, but sometimes she felt like a friend.
Sometimes the sweet smell of a cinnamon cupcake
Momentarily takes me back to sharing my story with her.

Those days, I was overwhelmed with heartbreak,
But now that terrible feeling is a blur.
I often wonder if things just happened to align
Or if this sacred relationship was God's good design.

The Story of My Hands

My hands tell a story
They tell of a toddler wanting to explore
Touching every toy and food
To learn about this big new world
They tell a story of a child's desire for victory
Making my best friend
Crown me the winner
Of Rock Paper Scissors
And when I won cheerleading competitions
They held up the shiny first-place trophy
And high-fived my teammates
They tell the story of love
As I comforted a carsick puppy
After she puked on my sister
The day we took her home
And rubbed the back of my grieving mother
As I hugged her seventeen years later
When that puppy passed away
They softly held my granny's bruised and skinny hand as I said goodbye
Before she left this world behind
They tell a story of teenage love
They started to sweat
When my high school crush put my hand in his
I thought they were so cool
When they did a special handshake with a football player
In those days, they told a story of a gal
Who just wanted to feel pretty
So one of them held a tube of mascara
While the other one placed the wand to my eyelashes
They held the flat iron as it straightened each strand of hair

And held the pack of 5 Gum as the guy
In seventh period (who liked to flirt) grabbed a piece
My hands tell a story of relationships
They shook the hands of pastors each Sunday
And bosses as I embarked on a journey of a new job
They tell a story of bravery
As they trembled while putting the key in the ignition
Of an old black 4Runner
The first day I ever drove
And staying raised the entire time
When I rode my first roller coaster
Because my youth pastor said I was too afraid to do it

You see, I didn't always think much of their stories
They were drowned out by the noise of trauma
And I didn't know the truth that the story never ended there
My hands told a chapter of tragedy
A chapter I would rather not read
They were forced to touch some things
That were never meant for them
And forced to carry the weight
Of another man's sin
But, friends, I learned that was only a chapter
A mere handful of pages
In the bigger story my hands can tell
They tell a story of redemption
As they raise and praise the Lord
Thanking Him for saving me and changing me
A story of minor mishaps
As they held the antihistamine
On the second date, where I learned I am allergic to cats
They tell a story of steadfastness
As they fold together to pray
For my dad's heart despite not seeing change
They tell a story of a gosh-darn rock star
As my right hand

Chose
To reach out to open that cold steel door handle of the state police station
The day after Christmas…with COVID-19
To fight for protection and justice

My hands tell a story
And it is not over yet
I will let them speak

Freedom

*F*erns line the houses I walk by on my way to work.
*R*ed cardinals and yellow butterflies help me
*E*njoy God's creation. The fragrance of the flowers
*E*ntice me to stop and smell them.
"*D*on't rush!" I remind myself and adjust my pace.
*O*h, my soul, this is the peace you were longing for.
*M*oment by moment, I live in the light of Jesus's love.

Learning to Live with a Father

My whole life, I have had a dad
But it wasn't until
My late twenties that I knew
What it was like to have a Father
Sure, I met the Father
At a small church in my hometown
When I was fifteen
But I just assumed
He was the same as Dad
But day by day, I learned
Just how much they weren't the same
I learned that I am allowed
To use the language of lament
I am allowed to cry out to my Father
And ask Him why He seems so far away
Or why things don't feel fair
It's okay to ask the Father why
He didn't take away my pain
Unlike Dad, He listens and cares
There's no need to push my feelings away
I even learned the Father has feelings too
He gets angry at the sin
Committed against me
He is hurt to see His daughter hurting
And it makes Him happy
When His child chooses to take the right path
He even wants to meet with me
For my morning cup of coffee
As the warmth of the liquid
Comes up to my lips

He wants me to enjoy it
And He wants to hear about my day
The Father wants me
To get to know Him better too
Unlike Dad, who wanted
Me not to touch the remote
When the Father corrects me
I am not left wondering
What I did wrong
Paralyzed with fear to take the next steps
Because I don't understand why I was wrong
Or how to do the right thing
Instead, I walk away thankful that the Father
Spared me from future pain
One day at a time, I learned that I love
To serve the Father
I like to simply make Him happy
By doing the things He'd want me to do
I love to tell people
Of this special relationship we have
And I'm glad to be a servant of my Father
Instead of a slave to my dad
I can't wait to learn more
About what it means
To live life with a Father

Life in Healing

When I wake up in the morning, I finally feel alive
I start my day slowly, just listening to the birds
Hearing their daily melody helps me thrive
Then I read and listen to my Father's holy words

I no longer see the world through a lens of fear
Now I can simply enjoy my Creator
My soul soaks up His creation, reminding me He's here
I was never meant to be a child of fear, I was meant for something greater

I learned that God has never left me
I was just blinded by my past
His Word and children helped me see
That He will always hold me fast

In this life, I may not be fully healed, but now I know the truth and lies
Thank you, my Lord, for slowly opening my eyes

About the Author

Emma Leigh Levine was born and raised in Southern West Virginia. She went to church her whole life but never truly experienced Jesus until high school. Unfortunately, God decided to draw her to Himself through trauma and tragedy. Emma loves to write about what Jesus has done through her experiences, both easy and difficult. In her poetry, she isn't afraid to ask God the hard questions or simply sit with her pain. Not every poem has a happy ending, but Jesus is good throughout all of them.

Emma took a creative writing class at Marshall University, where she received her undergrad degree. That is where she figured out that she likes writing poetry. She then took a poetry class where she fell in love with the art. Since then her love for poetry has flourished. During her time in grad school, she wrote a lot of poetry and shared with a couple of friends. They encouraged her and prayed for her in hopes that she would get the chance to share her art with more people.

Emma graduated from Southeastern Baptist Theological Seminary with a master's degree in Christian counseling. She hopes to share the love of God with suffering people and is excited to see the Lord change them. She can't wait to keep seeing God use the terrible parts of her story for His glory and her good!

When Emma isn't writing, she loves painting, baking, and being outdoors. Her house is filled with her own paintings. Seeing her art hanging on the wall makes her happy. Emma loves to bake! Her family always looks forward to her pumpkin bread and snickerdoodles at Thanksgiving. While she is clumsy, leading her to stay away from big hikes, Emma loves hiking small local trails with her friends and family. Being in nature makes her feel close to God.